WELCOME TO THERAPY

A MINDFUL INTRODUCTION TO COUNSELING FOR KIDS

ANDREA DORN, MSW, LISW-CP

Dedication

To those doing the important work of therapy
and to the helpers who support them.

A special thank you to these friends and
colleagues, both old and new: Christine Brudnicki,
Stephanie Nicolet, Julie Benware, and Ivey Drawdy

Welcome To Therapy
Copyright © 2024 Andrea Dorn

Published by:
PESI Publishing
3839 White Ave
Eau Claire, WI 54703

Illustrations: Andrea Dorn
Cover: Andrea Dorn
Layout: Andrea Dorn & Amy Rubenzer

ISBN: 9781683736875 (print)
ISBN: 9781683736882 (epub)
ISBN: 9781683736899 (ePDF)

PESI Publishing
pesipublishing.com

 Read Me First:

Welcome to the Mindful Steps Series! The book you're about to read is called a "process story." Process stories are incredible teaching tools that help caregivers and professionals:

- Share important, often abstract, concepts with children in a concrete way.
- Describe a new concept or skill to children while allowing them to process their feelings.
- Engage children in learning.
- Prompt important open-ended conversations with children to personalize the learning experience, build social-emotional skills, and strengthen connection and healthy attachment.

---

*Tip: This book is about more than just learning about what happens when you go to therapy. It's also about cultivating mindfulness, creating physical and emotional awareness, and practicing mindful language. Here are some tips to keep in mind to get the most out of this book:

- To reinforce social-emotional learning and body and emotion awareness, ask open-ended questions while reading each page. Use the suggested interactive prompts at the bottom of the pages (or create your own) to spark conversation. Depending on the age and development of your child, they may not always have the answers, but it will help to prime their mind and help them start thinking about the importance of these concepts.
- Familiarize yourself with the text and optional engagement questions by reading this book on your own before reading it with your child.
- Use validation and reflective listening to respond to any feelings or thoughts your child may share.
- Read this book all the way through or just focus on the parts that are important to reiterate with your child.
- Read this book at different stages throughout your child's time in therapy to reiterate the process and highlight progress.

Oh! Hi there! What is your name?

Really?! That is **MY** name too!

I am growing every day, and as I grow,
I get to learn lots of fun things!

Optional Questions: What fun things do you know how to do?
What new things would you like to learn or try?

Doing fun things
can be really great!

But sometimes tricky things happen, and I can start to feel stuck. Most of the time, I can work through tricky situations, but there are times when things happen and I need help getting unstuck.

Optional Questions: Can you share any tricky things you've worked through?
Is there anything tricky that is happening in your life right now?

I'm learning that tricky times are normal and happen to everyone. I am also learning that it is good to have help when things get tough.

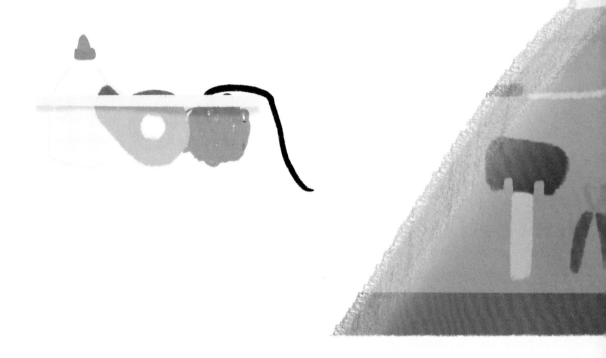

 Optional Questions: Who can you ask for help when things get a little tough? A lot tough?

When something *extra* tricky happens to me or my family, there are special grown-up helpers who are ready to help us work through these times. There are lots of types of grown-up helpers.

One type is called a **therapist** or **counselor**.
A therapist is a grown-up with a caring heart who helps people work through feelings when something in their life is tricky, scary, or not working quite right.

Kids and grown-ups all over the world
meet with therapist helpers.

Optional Questions: Do you know anyone who meets with a therapist helper?
Can you think of any other kinds of helpers?

When I meet with a therapist, it is called "going to therapy." Therapy is a safe and private place where kids can talk and play and learn ways to feel better when things get extra tricky.

Here is what happens when I go to therapy.

Optional Question: Do you know what "private" means?

First, I will meet my therapist. I will have a special therapist that's just for me.

Kids can have a lot of feelings about meeting someone new. Here are some feelings you might have when you meet a new person:

Excited

Shy

Silly

Nervous

Curious

Confident

Worried

Brave

Calm

 **Optional Questions:** How do you feel when you meet a new person?
Point to the feelings on the chart you have about meeting your therapist.
Do you know your therapist's name?

Usually, a therapist works in a room called an office, but sometimes a therapist or counselor will work at a school or even meet with you at your home.

I will meet with my therapist several times so I can get to know them and they can get to know me.

Optional Questions:
Where will you meet with your therapist?
Is there anything you'd like to know about your therapist?
What would you like your therapist to know about you?

After we get to know each other, we will work together on the things that are feeling tricky. To do this, we will play and sometimes talk.

My therapist is a great . . .

listener,

problem solver,

game player,

and feelings detective.

When we meet, my therapist and I will discover all kinds of things together. I will learn about myself, my feelings, and the tricky things I'm going through.

I'll learn to notice what I feel and think when something is tricky.

I'll also figure out what tools I can use to work through tricky times.

Do 10 jumping jacks

Spot one thing from each color of the rainbow

Talk to someone

Listen to my favorite song

Say something kind to myself

Take a break

Be curious about my feelings

Hug my favorite toy or blanket

Optional Question:

How does your body feel when something is tricky?
If you already know some tools that help you feel better,
you can create a toolbox and fill it with these tools.

I will learn that my therapist can help me through some of the toughest parts of my life.

My job is to do my best to share my thoughts and feelings and to be open to trying new things.

But it's also okay if I need a break sometimes. If I need a break from talking or playing, I can use my powerful words to tell my therapist, "I need a break." I get to be in charge of my body and my words when I'm in therapy.

 Optional Practice:

Let's practice asking for a break. Practice saying "I need a break" in a way that feels best for you. You can even try changing the pitch and tone of your voice to make it fun and silly. If saying "I need a break" feels tough, come up with a fun signal you can share with your caregiver or therapist so they know it's time for a break.

When I'm not at my therapist's office, I also have other people on my team who help me. My therapist may also talk with these people sometimes so they can help in the way that is best for me.

"Go, you!"

 Optional Question: Who is on your team? Let's make a list or draw a picture of your team together.

After going to therapy for a while, the things that were feeling tricky won't feel quite so tricky anymore. And one day, I will step out on my own ready to face the world through the happy times, the tough times, and all the times in between.

With a little help and the right tools, I will be able to work through anything. What I need will be found right inside of me, but I can always ask for help again if I need it.

Optional Question (when time in therapy is completed):
Who can you talk to if you think you may need to see a therapist again?

Sometimes life is fun, and sometimes it is tricky, but no matter what, there are always helpers there to help us find our way.

Thanks for spending time with me today!
See you next time!

Meditation for Children

Life is made for growing—I learn things every day.

But sometimes I get stuck and need some help along the way.

All of us need help at times, not only me or you.

Reaching out when things are tough can help to get us through.

When I'm feeling stuck or scared or notice I am down,

I can breathe and know that tools and helpers are around.

All I need to do is just take one step at a time.

When we work together, there is no hill we can't climb.

Caregiver Mindfulness Exercise

Supporting a child through intense emotions or challenging behaviors can be a demanding task for caregivers and professionals alike. I invite you to explore the following mindfulness exercise to help you engage with, and release the weight of, any difficult emotions you might be feeling in response to this experience. You can adapt this exercise to any setting and practice it whenever needed. If you find any part of this exercise distressing or unsettling, allow yourself permission to pause and take a break. You can always revisit it when you're ready.

To begin, find a comfortable position, either standing or sitting. Inhale deeply through your nose, allowing your eyes to gently close if that feels right to you. Shift your attention to the emotion you are currently sensing. Direct your focus inward, noticing where in your body this emotion is manifesting as well as the bodily sensations associated with it. How intense are these bodily sensations? Envision these emotions like waves, rising and eventually subsiding. Now, place your hands over your heart and silently repeat this affirmation to both yourself and the emotion: "You belong."

Especially for Caregivers, Teachers, and Therapists

Dear Reader,

If you are reading this book, you likely have a child who is, or work with children who are, seeking therapeutic or counseling services. Children and families benefit from therapy for a wide variety of reasons, and I am thankful for grown-ups like you who make mental health a priority for young minds.

How can this book help? This book helps children and families know what to expect when going to counseling and normalizes asking for help when we need it most. This book introduces the therapeutic process in a simple, developmentally appropriate, interactive, and neutral way. This allows a child's brain to be ready for what to expect, lets the child know what's expected of them, and allows room for the important discovery process that happens along the therapeutic journey.

If you've read any other books in the Mindful Steps Series, you'll notice this book doesn't specifically define mindfulness or provide a set of coping steps. Instead, it hints at the importance of being aware of your emotional and physical experience as you embark on the journey of reaching out for support, meeting someone new, and working through tricky times. It also focuses on the idea that children will discover new and exciting coping tools as they develop a partnership with their therapist.

I hope you find this book to be a positive addition to your child's therapeutic journey. From my heart to yours, thank you for being a part of supporting children in becoming their most emotionally healthy and thriving selves.

Happy reading and warmest regards,

Andrea

How to Best Support Your Child in Therapy

Prepare Your Child Ahead of Time

After you have made the decision to engage in therapy with your child and have found a therapist who is a good fit for your family, you can discuss this decision with your child. It can be most helpful to present this information in a simple and positive way. Using this book as a starting point can help guide and create meaningful discussions around what your child can expect as they begin therapy.

Use Helpful Language for Common Presenting Concerns

Sometimes, it can be difficult to know how to explain to a child why they may need to see a therapist. Simple, positive, and concrete explanations are usually best. Here are some helpful suggestions you can use while reading this book to help you better discuss any questions your child may have about why they are meeting with a therapist.

- **ADHD or attention difficulties:** "Everyone's brain works a little bit differently. Your brain has lots of energy and loves to be curious. Sometimes this can make it hard to focus on important things! A therapist can help you learn ways to focus when it feels tough."
- **Anxiety or OCD:** "When life gets tricky, it can sometimes make kids and grown-ups feel worried and nervous. A therapist can help you learn ways to help your body and mind feel calm and peaceful."
- **Behavioral struggles:** "Sometimes our brains and bodies can feel very busy, excited, and curious, and we might have a lot of energy. When this happens, it can be hard to focus and respect other people's space. A therapist can help you learn ways to feel calm and peaceful and to respect others."
- **Bullying or friendship concerns:** "Making friends and setting healthy boundaries can be tricky for kids and adults. A therapist can help you learn ways to find healthy friendships, stick up for what you think is right, and get help if you need it."

- **Depression:** "When life gets tricky, it can sometimes make kids and grown-ups feel sad. A therapist can help you learn ways to help your body and mind feel better."
- **Grief:** "When someone special dies, kids and adults can have a lot of tricky feelings. A therapist can help you learn ways to feel better and remember the person who died."
- **Trauma:** "When something scary happens, it can be tough on our bodies and minds. A therapist can help you work through tricky feelings and find ways to feel safe again after something scary happens."

Stay Engaged in the Therapy Process

Therapists will vary in the treatment methods they use, but it is usually most impactful if primary caregivers are involved and engaged in the therapeutic process. This may include being present for sessions, staying in contact with the therapist, keeping scheduled appointments, and being curious and open to the therapist's suggestions for best supporting your child. In some cases, engaging in family therapy may also be beneficial to your child's success.

Assist Your Child on Their Therapy Journey

Children are heavily influenced by the environments in which they spend most of their time. Supporting your child outside of the therapy room is just as important, if not more important, as the work being done in therapy. You can support your child by:

- **Listening to and validating their experience.** Therapy and life are a journey, and kids and adults alike need space to feel accepted and seen for their thoughts and feelings. Even if you don't always agree, do your best to acknowledge that your child's experience is true for them.
- **Guiding and modeling behaviors.** Children learn by watching the actions and reactions of their primary caregivers. If you model and reinforce the behaviors and coping skills your child is learning in therapy, you may see them pick these up even more quickly.

Explaining Privacy and Confidentiality in Therapy to Kids

A common question parents often ask is: "How much will my child's therapist share with me or others about their appointments?" The answer can vary depending on different factors and from one therapist to another. Regardless, most therapists are happy to share their confidentiality practices when you inquire about services, or they will go over this during the initial appointment.

Although therapy is a safe place where your child can share private information, there are times when therapists may need to share your child's confidential information with others. These times include if your child is going to seriously and imminently hurt themselves or someone else, or if your child reports that someone else is hurting them. Your therapist will be able to discuss these instances more in depth and answer any questions you may have.

Here are some important terms and their definitions to help explain privacy and confidentiality to children:

- **What is privacy?** Privacy means keeping your thoughts, feelings, and body to yourself and only sharing them with the people *you* choose.
- **What is confidentiality?** Confidentiality means keeping information private and not telling anyone else without permission.
- **What is permission?** Permission means telling someone it is okay to do something.

- **How do privacy, confidentiality, and permission work in therapy?** A therapist's job is to keep the things you talk about or do private and confidential. This means they will only share things you do or say with your permission. But there are a few times a therapist *may* talk to someone else about what you say. In these times, it is usually because it is important for them to help keep you or other people safe or because they need to share important information so other people can support you better. If you have any questions about what your therapist may need to talk to someone else about, you can ask your therapist or your caregiver to learn more.

Optional Questions:

Do you have any questions about what types of things your therapist might talk to other grown-ups about?

Do you have any questions about what it means to be safe?

Expanded Feelings Chart

Joy

Happy Excited Silly Peaceful Content Grateful

Empowerment

Brave Proud Confident Curious

Fear

Scared Worried Nervous Shy Embarrased

Expanded Feelings Chart

Anger

| Mad | Frustrated | Jealous | Disgusted |

Sadness

| Sad | Lonely | Hurt | Disappointed |

Other feelings

Surprised   Bored   Tired   Confused   Ashamed   Guilty

Author & Illustrator

Andrea Dorn, MSW, is a mom and licensed clinical social worker (LISW-CP) whose interest in mindfulness and behavioral and attachment theories began in graduate school. Since that time, Andrea has worked to incorporate the benefits of mindfulness into every aspect of her life and frequently uses behavioral and attachment theories to guide her clinical practice. She has found these theories, especially mindfulness, to be truly effective in transforming lives. She has also found clear, consistent, and attachment-based behavioral modification techniques to be crucial to developing healthy and thriving young minds.

The Mindful Steps series was inspired after a year of major transitions in Andrea's life with two young children in tow. Andrea found there was a lack of nonfiction, single-step resources for helping her own strong-willed child navigate and know what to expect during these big transitions. In order to fill this gap, she became interested in writing children's books and has discovered a true passion for the entire writing and publishing process.

What does this mean for you? It means that Andrea's work and writing is guided not only by her clinical and mindfulness background, but also by the care she takes in parenting with positivity, intentionality, and connection. She is dedicated to helping young minds learn techniques for calming their bodies and processing changes.

Andrea currently works in South Carolina as a psychotherapist with adults and children of all ages. In her free time, Andrea enjoys spending time with her family (husband, two kiddos, and dog), traveling, writing, dancing, and making meaningful connections with others. Please find Andrea on Instagram @mindfulstepsseries, Facebook @mindfulsteps, and YouTube @mindfulstepsseries.